Simple Solutions

House-Training

By Kim Campbell Thornton
Illustrations by Buck Jones

Plus Other Helpful Tips

BOWTIE
P R E S S®

IRVINE, CALIFORNIA

Ruth Strother, Project Manager
Nick Clemente, Special Consultant
Karla Austin, Editor; Michelle Martinez, Editorial Assistant
Michael Vincent Capozzi, Designer
Suzanne Gehrls, Production Manager

The dogs in this book are referred to as *he* and *she* in alternating chapters.

Library of Congress Cataloging-in-Publication Data

Thornton, Kim Campbell.
  House-training / by Kim Campbell Thornton ; illustrations by Buck Jones.
      p. cm. — (Simple solutions)
  ISBN 1-889540-84-6 (paperback : alk. paper)
  1. Puppies—Training. I. Title. II. SimpleSolutions.
  SF431 .T53 2002
  636.7'0887—dc21
                    2002005296

BowTie Press®
A Division of BowTie, Inc.
3 Burroughs
Irvine, California 92618

Printed and Bound in Singapore
10 9 8 7 6

Contents

The Secret to Successful House-Training

Puppies pee. And poop. A lot and often. If you've never lived with a puppy, you'd be amazed by the number of times the little furballs need to go potty. Every hour or two, they start sniffing and circling, looking for a place to do their business. If owners aren't watchful, accidents can frequently happen.

Not surprisingly, house-training is the first lesson new owners want to teach their pups, and rightfully so: House-

training is the foundation for good behavior. Without it,

dogs can't become members of the family, and they run

the risk of being exiled to the backyard, never getting the

attention and social interaction that they need and deserve.

Happily, the secrets to successful house-training are simple: Time, patience, consistency, and supervision are all that's needed. Puppies are quick learners. A regular potty schedule, combined with praise for going in the right spot, and they'll soon get the idea. Dogs are naturally clean animals, and they don't want to soil their living area. House-training teaches dogs that the house is the living area and the yard (or whatever spot you choose) is the potty area.

How Long Does it Take?

Just as with children, potty training a puppy is a process. It's not something a puppy can learn in a day, or even a week. While it might take only a few weeks for your dog to understand what you want, until she's four to six months old, she's not physiologically capable of "holding it" for more than about four to six hours. A dog's muscle control isn't fully developed, and her bladder is not large enough to "hold it" any longer than that.

Remember that each dog is an individual. Some pups

are potty trained at three months, while others may not be completely reliable until they're nine months to one year old.

A number of breeds are more difficult to house-train than others, including: many toy breeds, such as Chihuahuas, Yorkies, papillons, Chinese cresteds, Italian greyhounds, shih tzus, and poodles, especially the smaller ones; the bichon breeds, such as bichon frise, Maltese, Havanese, and Bolognese; various hounds, including bea-gles, Afghan hounds, salukis, harriers and foxhounds; Jack Russell terriers; and soft-coated wheaten terriers. These

dogs need extra supervision and a lot of positive rein-forcement.

If you acquire your puppy at eight weeks of age, expect to take her out at least six to eight times a day. By the time she's about six months old, potty trips will be down to three or four times a day. A rule of thumb is to take your puppy out in hourly intervals equal to her age in months. For instance, a two-month-old puppy should go out every two hours, a four-month-old every four hours, and a six-month-old every six hours. This can vary, of course, depending on the individual dog: Some young puppies need to go out every half-hour. It's your responsibility to make sure your pup gets plenty of opportunities to go potty in the right spot.

Other good rules to follow include taking your pup out first thing in the morning—yes, even before you have your first cup of coffee—and ten to thirty minutes after every meal, when she wakes from a nap, after every playtime, and the last thing at night, just before she goes to bed.

That's a lot of dog walks. What if everyone in your family works or goes to school? Those things are important but so is your puppy's potty schedule, especially for the first

couple of weeks she's with you. Without a schedule, your puppy can't learn what she needs to know. Try to get home once or twice during the day, hire a dog walker or pet sitter, or ask a friend or neighbor to take your dog out. Try taking time off work during the first week of house-training to firmly establish the schedule and rules in your pup's mind. It's helpful to start training on a weekend or during a long holiday.

How Do I House-Train My Puppy?

Start house-training your puppy as soon as you get him home. Even before you bring him into the house for the first time, take him to the potty spot you've chosen, and let him sniff around. Make note of any patterns of sniffing, circling, and squatting. These are his clues that he needs to go out. If he performs, praise him in a happy tone of voice, "Good potty!" Then take him inside, and introduce him to his special place, which can be a crate.

Dogs develop preferences for certain potty surfaces, usually based on what they learn as a puppy. It's a good idea to expose your pup to different potty surfaces such as asphalt, concrete, and gravel so that if you don't have access to grass, you won't have a problem getting him to go.

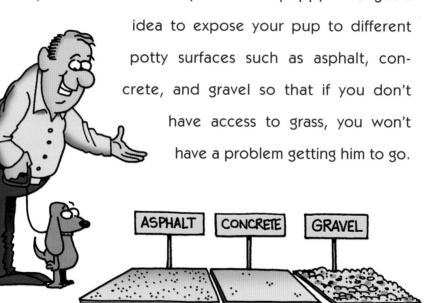

Young puppies should not have the run of the house. Before you bring your puppy home, choose a safe area of the house to let your pup stay. This is usually a kitchen, laundry room, bathroom, or some other area with an uncarpeted floor. Rooms with tile, vinyl, or concrete floors are good choices.

Lay down papers in this room (this is not paper-training but simply an easier way to clean up messes). Put your pup's open crate, a couple of chew toys, and a food and water dish at the opposite end of the room. Close off the room with a baby gate or other barrier to prevent him

from wandering throughout the house. Until your puppy is house-trained, he needs to be under your direct supervision or confined to an area where he can't get into trouble.

The goal is for your pup to eliminate away from his crate and eating area whenever you aren't there to take him out. Once your pup is consistently eliminating in a certain spot on the papers, you can gradually take up the papers, leaving only the favored area covered.

If you come home and your pup has pottied in the safe room, don't scold him. He's just doing what comes naturally. Take him outside and praise him when he potties in the chosen spot. If you take him to the same area every time, the lingering scent will prompt him to go again.

It's Cold Outside. Can I Paper-Train Her First?

Most trainers agree that teaching a puppy to go on paper and then retraining her to go outside can be confusing. Some dogs never quite figure out that they are supposed to move on from papers to the great outdoors and continue to potty on any pile of papers they see. One puppy who had been reliable in the house for some time had a relapse one day when her owners were painting the hall. They had laid down papers to protect the carpet,

and she came along and squatted on them for a quick pee. They hadn't paper-trained her at all, but apparently the breeder had laid down papers to protect her floors and the smart pup remembered what they were for. But if you live in a high-rise building or are unable to walk your dog regularly, try paper-training or litter box training.

To paper-train your dog, spread a few layers of paper in the area you want your pup to go. Then, instead of taking her outside, take her to the papers. Let her sniff around, but if she moves off the papers, set her back on them. When she eliminates, praise her.

If you're having trouble getting your pup to use the papers, try this trick. When she urinates, hold a sponge underneath the flow to capture some of the urine. You can then use the sponge to scent the papers. The next time you take your pup to the papers, she'll smell the urine and remember what she's supposed to do. You can also purchase pads at pet supply stores that claim to induce eliminating. When the pad is placed on the papers its scent is supposed to encourage a puppy to eliminate there. It's worth a try if you're having problems.

To house-train your dog with a litter box instead of papers, follow the same process as paper-training. Litter boxes and litter suited for puppies and dogs who weigh up to thirty-five pounds can be found in pet supply stores. Shredded paper, which some dogs prefer, can be substituted for litter.

Reward Performance

After your puppy eliminates, say, "Good potty!" or something else that comes across as praise. Choose any short phrase that works for you, and say it in a happy, approving tone of voice. When you assign a name to the action, your puppy learns to associate the word with the act and may learn to go on command. Just don't make the mistake one owner did of using the phrase "Good dog" or your pup will start going potty every time you praise him, whether you meant him to or not. Make sure everyone in the family knows the key phrase for going potty and uses

it consistently. You don't want your puppy to become confused.

Speed up the training process by making potty time pleasant for your puppy. Keep some tiny treats in your pocket so you can reward him the instant he's through eliminating (don't interrupt him before he's finished). Then, spend a few minutes playing. He'll soon learn that the quicker he does his business the sooner playtime comes. This is useful on rainy days or when you're in a hurry.

The Benefits of a Crate

Dogs are den animals, which means they like small, cozy spots such as the caves of their wild ancestors where they can curl up and feel safe. Since most of us can't provide caves for our dogs, a wire or plastic carrier, or crate, is the next best thing.

Many people don't like the idea of putting their puppy in something that looks like a cage. It seems cruel to them, but just the opposite is true. Placing your puppy in a crate when you can't be there to watch her keeps her safe and out of trouble. When she's in her crate, she can't nibble on the wallpaper, pee on your favorite rug, or get into the trash. That means you won't come home and get mad at her for doing what puppies do: explore, destroy, chew, and eliminate. Some people even place a dog crate or puppy playpen in several different rooms, such as the living room, bedroom, and home office, so that the puppy always has a safe place to be when she's not being watched.

Your job is to reduce your puppy's chances of making a mistake, and a crate is a good way to accomplish that. Using a crate is much kinder than banishing a dog to the

basement, garage, or backyard so that she never learns

how to be responsible in the house, and the cost of a

crate is much less than the cost of repairing chewed-up woodwork or furniture.

A crate should be just large enough for your dog to stand up, turn around, and stretch out on her side. If the crate is too big, your pup will be able to eliminate at one end of the crate and sleep at the other. If your little puppy is going to grow into a large adult, buy a crate suited to her adult size, but block off part of it with a box or divider. As your pup grows, you can increase the amount of space she has in the crate until a divider is no longer needed.

To teach your puppy that the crate is a happy place, give her a treat each time she goes inside. As she steps inside, say, "Crate!" or "Bed!" in a happy tone of voice. It's always a good idea to assign a name to each action you want your puppy to learn. Soon, she'll go racing to her crate whenever you say the magic word. Be sure to reward her with praise and a treat, and leave a safe chew toy inside for her to play with. Place the crate in a busy area of the house such as the den or kitchen so she doesn't feel abandoned when she's in it. You can feed your puppy meals in the crate, which is also a good way

to increase your pup's positive association with the crate.

Keep in mind that crates can be misused. Your pup should not be confined to her crate for more than three or four hours at a time during the day. It is cruel to leave a young pup in a crate all day long when no one is at home. It's counterproductive and leaves your puppy no choice but to eliminate in her crate, which defeats the crate's role in house-training. The crate is meant to be your pup's den area, and if she learns to soil the crate, it will be even more difficult to house-train her. (Be aware that crate-training often does not work with puppies from pet stores because they have learned that eliminating in a cage is normal.) If you have to leave your pup for an extended period of time, put the open crate in a safe room as described above.

It's important, too, that the crate not be used as a place of punishment. Never crate your puppy in anger. Her crate should always be a safe haven she can go to for a nap or to get away from the tugging fingers of toddlers. Be sure your children know that the crate is Daisy's special room, where she's not to be bothered.

At night, let your pup sleep in her crate next to your

bed. She'll be comforted by your presence, and in the morning, you'll be aware of any restlessness indicating she's ready to go out. It's important to avoid teaching your puppy that whining or barking will get her released from the crate. Wait until she's quiet before opening the door. She should be able to go the entire night without an accident, especially if she's more than three months old. (If your pup does need to go out in the middle of the night, put her right back in her crate after she has performed so she learns that nighttime isn't playtime.)

Preventing Potty Problems

Watching your puppy when he's outside his safe place is crucial. If you don't watch him, you won't be able to prevent accidents. A good way to keep your puppy from wandering off and having an accident while your back is turned is to leash him and keep him at your side. He'll enjoy being with you, and you'll notice immediately if he needs to go out. Give him a toy to play with while he's next to you. If you're doing something that doesn't allow you to keep a close watch on your puppy, put him in his crate, playpen, or safe room. This will help prevent any accidents.

Every time you notice your puppy sniffing, circling, or squatting, clap your hands to get his attention and, say, "Outside? Do you need to go outside?" Then hustle him out before he has a chance to do anything. Set a timer so that you remember to take him out every hour or two, even if he doesn't show any signs of needing to go out. Always take your pup out on a leash so you can see him potty, and praise him when he does. Giving a small food reward, such as a bit of kibble, immediately after your pup

potties further reinforces the habit of eliminating outdoors.

Consistent positive reinforcement is the key to successful house-training.

It's very important that you go outside with your puppy. If you aren't there with him, you can't praise him for eliminating or teach him the *go potty* command. You also have no way of knowing whether he actually did anything. Many pet owners get angry because they send their pup outside and then the pup pees or poops when he comes inside. Without your guidance, your pup doesn't know why he's outside. If he hasn't performed after fifteen or twenty minutes, take him inside and crate him. Try again later.

What Goes in Must Come Out

Another way to help your puppy potty on schedule is to feed her at set times each day rather than leaving food out and allowing her to nibble all day long. When your dog eats at the same times every day, it's easier to gauge when she'll need to go out. Feed your young pup after her first elimination of the day, once in midafternoon, and again in the evening, spacing her meals about six hours apart. Feeding your pup high-quality, highly digestible food helps keep her on schedule as well. The ingredients in these foods produce less stool volume, meaning your puppy won't have to eliminate as often.

Eating stimulates your pup's bowels, so take her outside after every meal. Give her a couple of minutes to do her business and if she doesn't potty, take her back inside and crate her so that she doesn't potty in the house. Try again in ten minutes. Keep taking her out at ten-minute intervals until she performs, paying attention to the amount of time that elapses between the end of the meal and when she finally potties. Most pups need to go thirty to sixty minutes

after eating. If you know your pup's needs, you can keep

her on schedule and avoid accidents.

Accidents Happen

Your puppy is bound to make mistakes, especially in the first few weeks of house-training. Always remember that he is just a baby—no matter what his size—and that he needs time to learn. You are his teacher, and he relies on you to make sure that he gets plenty of opportunities to do things right.

If your pup pees or poops in the house, don't yell at him. Instead, make a note to yourself to watch him more closely and take him out more frequently. Then gently put

HONEY, ACTUALLY, SHE IS STILL A PUPPY.

him in his crate or the safe room, and clean up the mess. Remember: reward correct behavior and ignore unwanted behavior. Never rub his nose in the mess or swat him with a rolled-up newspaper, or anything else. Not only will anger and punishment increase stress and fear in your puppy, but he'll also become sneaky about finding places to potty.

If you catch your puppy in the act of eliminating in the house, clap your hands to get his attention and, say, "Aaaaght Outside." If he stops (unlikely), take him outside to finish. Avoid saying "No" or calling him a bad dog. You don't want him to think that the act of eliminating is wrong, you just want him to know that he chose the wrong place.

Until your pup is reliable, don't let him run free in your home. A puppy who is eliminating everywhere in the house has too much freedom. Instead, keep him by your side or confined to his safe room or crate. This is especially important during busy times of the day such as mornings and dinnertime, when you have less time to watch him. It is important to restrict his access to certain areas within the house until he starts eliminating outdoors on a regular basis.

Part of house-training is being able to read your pup's cues. Dogs have different ways of letting you know when they need to go out. Some dogs bark or run to the door, but others are subtle in their communications, which they limit to staring or twitching their ears a certain way. Many dogs learn to ring a bell when they want to go out. To teach this trick, hang a bell on the doorknob or on the wall next to the door. Be sure it's within your pup's reach. Every time you take him out for a potty run, ring the bell

before you go out the door. When he rings the bell on his

own, praise him and take him out. Whatever the sound or

behavior, watch your pup closely to learn his signals.

If you're having problems house-training your puppy, make sure you're being consistent with your training methods. Don't try method after method, quickly switching from one to another. Choose the method you want to use, and stick with it. Otherwise, your pup will become confused. Keep in mind, too, that house-training accidents—especially after a pup seems reliable—may indicate a health problem. Take your puppy to a veterinarian for an exam if he suddenly breaks house-training for no apparent reason. He may have a bladder or kidney infection.

Cleaning Up

There's a technique to removing stains and odors caused by puppy waste. If done properly, your carpet can look and smell as good as new.

When you're dealing with urine, the first step is to sop up as much of the liquid as possible. Keep a supply of ratty old towels on hand for this job. When you've absorbed as much moisture as possible, saturate the spot with the cleanser of your choice. Many pet owners find success using products such as Resolve, OdorMute,

Nature's Miracle, Simple Solution, and Anti-Icky-Poo. Others simply use white vinegar. Avoid using ammonia or any cleansers that contain ammonia; ammonia is a component of urine, and its scent will draw your pup back to that spot again and again.

Once you've applied the cleanser, use a clean towel or rag to blot the area again. Then get a dry towel, place it over the area, and pile some heavy books on top of it. No, your puppy won't read them while she's on the toilet, but the weight of the books presses the towel into the carpet drawing out more moisture. Leave the books on the spot

overnight or until the area is dry. Sprinkle the spot with baking powder to help wick away moisture and vacuum it up when the spot is dry. You can soak up moisture with a wet vacuum, too.

If you can smell that your pup has had an accident but can't find the spot, use a black light to find the stain on the carpet. Saturate the area with your chosen cleanser and follow the steps described above.

For solid waste, use a towel or rag to pick up as much of the mess as possible. Dump the stool in the toilet, and toss the towel in a bucket for a hot-water wash later on.